RENEGADE GOSPEL
LEADER GUIDE

Renegade Gospel
The Rebel Jesus

Book
978-1-4267-9279-3
978-1-4267-9280-9 eBook

DVD
978-1-4267-9282-3

Leader Guide
978-1-4267-9281-6
978-1-63088-037-8 eBook

Youth Study Book
978-1-4267-9283-0
978-1-4267-9284-7 eBook

Children's Leader Guide
978-1-4267-9285-4

For more information, visit www.MikeSlaughter.com

Also by Mike Slaughter

Dare to Dream

shiny gods

Christmas Is Not Your Birthday

Change the World

Spiritual Entrepreneurs

Real Followers

Momentum for Life

UnLearning Church

Upside Living in a Downside Economy

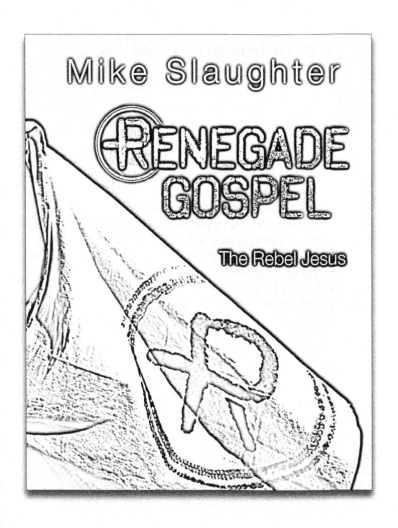

Mike Slaughter

RENEGADE GOSPEL

The Rebel Jesus

LEADER GUIDE

by Martha Bettis Gee

Abingdon Press / Nashville

RENEGADE GOSPEL: THE REBEL JESUS

Leader Guide
by Martha Bettis Gee

Copyright © 2014 Abingdon Press
All rights reserved.

This book is printed on elemental chlorine-free paper.

ISBN 978-1-4267-9281-6

Scripture quotations unless noted otherwise are from the Holy Bible, New International Version®, NIV®. Copyright © 1973, 1978, 1984, 2011 by Biblica, Inc.™ Used by permission of Zondervan. All rights reserved worldwide. www.zondervan.com. The "NIV" and "New International Version" are trademarks registered in the United States Patent and Trademark Office by Biblica, Inc.™

The Scripture quotation marked CEB is taken from the Common English Bible. Copyright © 2011 by the Common English Bible. All rights reserved. Used by permission. www.CommonEnglishBible.com.

14 15 16 17 18 19 20 21 22 23—10 9 8 7 6 5 4 3 2 1

MANUFACTURED IN THE UNITED STATES OF AMERICA

CONTENTS

TO THE LEADER

Welcome! In this study, you have the opportunity to help a group of learners as they reexamine their response to Jesus' invitation, "Come and follow me." As pastor and author Mike Slaughter points out, it doesn't take much commitment simply to profess one's belief in Jesus Christ. It is a far different matter, however, to take seriously Jesus' words, "Whoever wants to be my disciple must deny themselves and take up their cross daily and follow me" (Luke 9:23).

In this Lenten study, Slaughter invites learners to join him in challenging the illusions many of us have constructed of a benign, Sunday school Jesus who only taught us nice ways to live and who exists to serve our personal needs and take us to heaven. Over the course of the study, learners will encounter the rebel Jesus, who came to initiate a revolutionary movement to bring God's kingdom into the world. In the process, they will be encouraged to consider what it means to follow such a Savior, and what the true cost of discipleship is.

Expelling illusions and reshaping perceptions can be risky work. Some participants may find this study unsettling. The idea of a rebel Jesus initiating a revolutionary movement may make them uncomfortable or even a little angry. Consider how to create the kind of learning environment where participants can confront their own assumptions and express their thoughts and feelings honestly, as well as listen to others with sensitivity.

Scripture tells us that where two or three are gathered together, we can be assured of the presence of the Holy Spirit, working in and through all those gathered. As you prepare to lead, pray for that presence and expect that you will experience it.

This six-session study makes use of the following components:

- the study book, *Renegade Gospel: The Rebel Jesus*, by Mike Slaughter;
- this Leader Guide;
- the video segments that accompany the study.

Participants in the study will also need Bibles, as well as either a spiral-bound notebook for a journal or an electronic means of journaling, such as a tablet. If possible, notify those interested in the study in advance of the first session. Make arrangements for them to get copies of the book so that they can read the Introduction and Chapter 1.

Using This Guide with Your Group

Because no two groups are alike, this guide has been designed to give you flexibility and choice in tailoring the sessions for your group. The session format is listed below. You may choose any or all of the activities, adapting them as you wish to meet the schedule and needs of your particular group.

In many cases your session time will be too short to do all the activities. Select ahead of time which activities the group will do, for how long, and in what order. In some sessions, online video clips of music selections are suggested. While these clips can give participants a multisensory experience of the music, they are not essential to the study.

In some sessions Bible study and book study are separate segments, while in others Bible study and book study are combined. In either case, you will be presented with a variety of activities to choose from. Depending on which activities you select, there may be special preparation needed. The leader is alerted to what is needed up front in the session plan.

Session Format

Planning the Session
    Session Goals
    Biblical Foundation
    Special Preparation
Getting Started
    Opening Activity
    Opening Prayer
Learning Together
    Video Study and Discussion
    Book Study and Discussion
    Bible Study and Discussion
Wrapping Up
    Closing Activity
    Closing Prayer

Helpful Hints

Preparing for the Session

- Pray for the leading of the Holy Spirit as you prepare for the study. Pray for discernment for yourself and for each member of the study group.
- Before each session, familiarize yourself with the content. Read the book chapter again.
- Choose the session elements you will use during the group session, including the specific discussion questions you plan to cover. Be prepared, however, to adjust the session as group members interact and as questions arise. Prepare carefully, but allow space for the Holy Spirit to move in and through the group members and through you as facilitator.
- If you plan to use online clips, obtain a video projector for the duration of the study. Persons with smartphones can access the clips in that way, but this is less effective with music videos.

- Prepare the space where the group will meet so that the space will enhance the learning process. Ideally, group members should be seated around a table or in a circle so that all can see each other. Movable chairs are best, because the group will often be forming pairs or small groups for discussion.
- Bring a supply of Bibles for those who forget to bring their own. Having a variety of translations is helpful.
- For most sessions you will also need a chalkboard and chalk, a whiteboard and markers, or an easel with paper and markers.

Shaping the Learning Environment

- Begin and end on time.
- Create a climate of openness, encouraging group members to participate as they feel comfortable. As mentioned above, some participants may find this study unsettling and may be uncomfortable or even angry. Be on the lookout for signs of discomfort in those who may be silent, and encourage them to express their thoughts and feelings honestly.
- Remember that some people will jump right in with answers and comments, while others need time to process what is being discussed.
- If you notice that some group members seem never to be able to enter the conversation, ask them if they have thoughts to share. Give everyone a chance to talk, but keep the conversation moving. Moderate to prevent a few individuals from doing all the talking.
- Communicate the importance of group discussions and group exercises.
- If no one answers at first during discussions, do not be afraid of silence. Count silently to ten, then say something such as, "Would anyone like to go first?" If no one responds, venture an answer yourself and ask for comments.

- Model openness as you share with the group. Group members will follow your example. If you limit your sharing to a surface level, others will follow suit.
- Encourage multiple answers or responses before moving on to the next discussion question or exercise.
- Ask, "Why?" or "Why do you believe that?" or "Can you say more about that?" to help continue a discussion and give it greater depth.
- Affirm others' responses with comments such as "Great" or "Thanks" or "Good insight"—especially if it's the first time someone has spoken during the group session.
- Monitor your own contributions. If you are doing most of the talking, back off so that you do not train the group to listen rather than speak up.
- Remember that you do not have all the answers. Your job is to keep the discussion going and encourage participation.

Managing the Session

- Honor the time schedule. If a session is running longer than expected, get consensus from the group before continuing beyond the agreed-upon ending time.
- Involve group members in various aspects of the group session, such as saying prayers or reading the Scripture.
- Note that the session guides sometimes call for breaking into smaller groups or pairs. This gives everyone a chance to speak and participate fully. Mix up the groups; don't let the same people pair up for every activity.
- As always in discussions that may involve personal sharing, confidentiality is essential. Group members should never pass along stories that have been shared in the group. Remind the group members at each session: confidentiality is crucial to the success of this study.

1.

DISCOVERING THE
REBEL JESUS

Planning the Session

Session Goals

As a result of conversations and activities connected with this session, group members should begin to:

- examine the portrait of Jesus often presented in the church and compare it with the Jesus revealed in Scripture;
- encounter some of the stories and teachings of Jesus presented in the gospels;
- explore four compelling and challenging identities of Jesus;
- embark on an exploration to rediscover the rebel Jesus;
- recommit to journey with Jesus as disciples.

Biblical Foundation

Jesus answered, "I am the way and the truth and the life." (John 14:6)

Special Preparation

- If possible in advance of the first session, ask participants to bring either a spiral-bound notebook or an electronic means of journaling such as a tablet. Provide writing paper and pens for those who may need them. Also have Bibles for those who do not bring one.

- Gather some images of Jesus—framed pictures found in your church school rooms, curriculum pictures, or images from the Internet. Set up a display of pictures around your learning space, or plan to project digital images for the group. If possible, include Warner Sallman's "Head of Christ," the image to which the author refers.

- Locate a small cross to display for the duration of the study. Choose a simple cross constructed of wood rather than a more ornate or decorative example, or use a picture of a cross.

- On a large sheet of paper or a board, print the following: "As I think back on my early experiences at church, I picture Jesus as …"

- On another sheet or board in another location, print the following: Warner Sallman's "Head of Christ"; John Perkins, Tom Skinner, Juan Carlos Ortiz, Tony Campolo; Uncle Gilbert; high school rock band; University of Cincinnati.

- Also read over the material in Chapter 1 in which Slaughter reviews some of Jesus' teachings. Depending on the size of your group, post some or all of the following Scripture references: Mark 1:21-28; John 5:1-9; Luke 17:11-19; John 2:13-16; Matthew 5:21-22; 27-28; 31-32; 40-42; Luke 9:23-24; Mark 10:17-22; John 6:60-66; Luke 14:25-33; Matthew 20:1-16, 20-25; Matthew 22:34-40; Matthew 26:47-56.

- Remember that there are more activities than most groups will have time to complete, As leader, you'll want to go over the session in advance and select or adapt the activities you think will work best for your group in the time allotted.

Getting Started

Opening Activity

As participants arrive, welcome them to the study. Invite them to view the images of Jesus Christ you have on display or you have projected digitally. If group members are not familiar with one another, make nametags available. Provide Bibles for those who did not bring one.

When most participants have arrived, ask them to form pairs. Invite pairs to introduce themselves if they are not acquainted, respond to the posted prompt, and discuss their responses with their partner. ("As I think back on my early experiences at church, I picture Jesus as . . .") After a few minutes, gather together. Invite volunteers to tell how they pictured Jesus. Discuss:

- What do these images communicate to you about who Jesus is?
- How would you describe what the author calls the "Sunday school Jesus"?

If they have not already done so, invite group members to silently read the Introduction in the study book. Discuss:

- Mike Slaughter, the author, suggests that we have taken the Jesus of history and recreated him to reflect our own cultural, political, ideological, and denominational perspectives. Do you agree or disagree, and why?
- What is your response to the last paragraph of the Introduction, in which the author characterizes Jesus not as a benign Savior but as a rebel who came to initiate the revolutionary movement of God? How closely does this picture of Jesus mesh with the way you have experienced him? Does it intrigue you? Does it make you uncomfortable? Why?
- The author observes that discipleship begins not with one's profession of faith but in the commitment to make a journey with Jesus. He quotes Will Willimon and Stanley Hauerwas, who write that we cannot know Jesus without

following Jesus. How do you respond to this statement about following Jesus? How closely does it reflect how you have experienced your faith journey?

Invite a volunteer to read aloud that last paragraph in the Introduction. As you begin this study, ask the group to reflect on the two contrasting views of Jesus the author presents here, and to invite the Spirit to open their minds and hearts to fresh understandings of who Jesus is. Also point out the cross you have displayed in the meeting space. During Lent, we are reminded that the journey with Jesus leads to a cross. Explain that for the duration of the study, this cross will serve as a reminder of the true cost of discipleship.

Opening Prayer

As we begin the season of Lent, O God, we seek to more faithfully follow the Jesus revealed in the Scriptures and to truly know him. Strip away our conceptions of a benign Savior. Make us aware in new ways that the journey with Jesus leads to a cross. In the name of Jesus Christ we pray. Amen.

Learning Together

Video Study and Discussion

The Session 1 video explores the difference between the real, resurrected Jesus and the Jesus of our imaginations. Briefly introduce Mike Slaughter, the book author and video presenter, using the profile found at http://ginghamsburg.org/bring/our-pastors/mike-slaughter.

Before viewing the video, remind participants of the images of Jesus they just viewed. Invite them to bring to mind the image of Jesus they carry from their early years in Sunday school. Tell them that in the video segments, they will hear Mike Slaughter fielding questions from members of the congregation he serves, Ginghamsburg Church.

- In response to a question, Slaughter describes how he first encountered the rebel Jesus. What was powerful for him about the people his uncle invited to table to break bread together with him?
- One questioner is curious about how Slaughter came to title his book. Why does he say that his congregation is not of the Democratic or Republican or Tea Party kingdom?
- Slaughter comments that he can't feed people, but he can show them the menu. What does his statement mean?

Invite the group to continue to reflect on what they saw and heard in the video. Encourage them to think about questions they might have asked if given the opportunity and to jot these down in their journals.

Book Study and Discussion

The Decline of Christianity

In Chapter 1, Slaughter observes that the fastest-growing religion in America is "no religion" and that as the commitment to Christianity has declined, Islam has become increasingly more attractive to Americans. Invite the group to discuss the following:

- The author suggests that this decline can be attributed in part to the fact that we have "dumbed down" what it means to be a disciple of Christ. How do you respond? Would you agree or disagree? Why?
- What does Slaughter mean when he says that we have turned "church" into a noun?

Call the group's attention to Slaughter's wry name for the congregation in which he grew up: "First Church of the Frozen Chosen." Ask them to think about their childhood church home. What name best describes that congregation? How might they characterize this congregation of which they are members now? Invite volunteers to tell the names they might choose.

Charting a Faith Journey

Woven into this first chapter is Mike Slaughter's account of his own early faith journey. If they have not already had a chance to do so, invite participants to read this account silently (book Chapter 1 in the section "A Subversive Movement," beginning "My initial discovery . . ."). After allowing a few minutes' reading time, call their attention to the list you have posted containing names and terms from Slaughter's account. Ask volunteers to explain the relevance of each item in the list to Slaughter's faith journey.

Invite group members to consider their own faith journeys up to this point in their lives. Ask them to make a similar list in their journals of events or people who have shaped their faith in significant ways. Invite volunteers to name one event or person they listed and explain why that person or event was significant for them. Then ask each person to reflect on where they are currently in terms of their faith and to consider the questions Slaughter poses about his own faith:

- Have I become too comfortable?
- Have I fallen into the spiritual poverty of wealth (or of aspiring to more material success)?

Encourage them to consider these questions, to ask themselves what other roadblocks are inhibiting their own spiritual growth, and to make note of the roadblocks in their journals.

Bible Study and Discussion

Explore Some Revolutionary Teachings of Jesus

Slaughter relates a personal turning point in his own faith journey—a time when as a teenager he felt compelled to pull out the Bible he had previously not studied and began to read the Gospels. He notes that the Jesus he encountered bore no resemblance to the fairy tale Jesus he had heard about in Sunday school.

He challenges us to explore how Jesus is presented in the "red letters," referring to the fact that some Bibles print the words of Jesus in red type.

Invite participants to explore some of Jesus' teachings. Depending on the size of your group, form pairs to explore some of the passages you posted, or assign passages to individuals. Explain that the passages in many cases are expanded beyond the verses cited in the book so that they can get a sense of the context of the verse. Ask them to read the verses, as well as Slaughter's commentary on the passage, and to discuss with their partner. Afterward, ask each pair to relate one insight from their passage to the larger group. Discuss:

- What words would you use to describe the Jesus revealed in these passages?
- Although Jesus challenged his followers, then and now, to pursue seemingly impossible standards, there was a key difference between Jesus and the Pharisees. What was it?

Discover Four Identities of Jesus in Scripture

In the book, four names are given by which Jesus is frequently identified in Scripture: Son of God, Son of Man, Servant of All, and Savior of the World. Form four smaller groups and give each group a large sheet of paper and markers. Assign one of the identifiers of Jesus to each small group. Invite them to read the portion of the book in which each name is discussed. Ask group members to discuss and then respond in writing on the sheet to the following:

- This name for Jesus conveys the following about who Jesus is …
- Identifying Jesus in this way adds to my understanding of Jesus by …
- In my own experience, seeing Jesus in this way helps me by …
- I have these questions about naming Jesus in this way …

When groups have had a chance to work, ask them to post their papers on the wall at intervals around your space. Have a spokesperson for each group report their group's discussion. Then invite the group to reflect in silence on the four names. Call for class members to respond out loud with the following:

- the name with which they most resonate;
- how the four names relate to one another to form a more complete picture of Jesus.

Commit to Lenten Disciplines

Slaughter challenges us to reread—or read for the first time—one of the four Gospels. Encourage group members to take this on as a Lenten discipline. Suggest the following plan:

- If persons have never read one of the Gospels in its entirety, suggest that they read the Gospel of Mark, the earliest of the Gospel accounts.
- If they have read one or more Gospel accounts, encourage them to choose one of the three so-called Synoptic Gospels—Matthew, Mark, or Luke—to reread now. These three Gospels are referred to as synoptic because they are so similar in structure, content, and wording, although each one has some content not found in the others. Invite participants to compare what they are reading with John's account of Jesus' arrest, crucifixion, and resurrection (the most important part of the gospel story).

An alternate plan might be to have first-time readers read Mark, and then to assign one of the Synoptic Gospels to the remaining group members. Ask volunteers also to read John's Gospel. In any case, invite the group to keep in mind these questions:

- How is Jesus presented in this Gospel that is different from your initial impression?

- What is Jesus, as presented in this Gospel, calling you to be and do?

Wrapping Up

Closing Activity

According to Slaughter, the crowds who came to hear Jesus were motivated by self-interest, miracles of healing, and free food. But Jesus reminded them to count the cost of discipleship. Ask:

- What would you name as equivalent reasons that people show up today for church?
- In what ways do our lives in institutional churches compare with the revolution that the rebel Jesus came to start?
- To what extent, if at all, do we reflect that countercultural community of people Slaughter identifies as church?

Encourage class members to reflect in the days ahead on the degree to which they are comfortable with the potential cost of being the kind of disciples we are called to be.

- What would we need to change in our individual lives?
- How might this congregation be shaped differently by answering such a call?

Remind group members to read Chapter 2 before the next session.

Closing Prayer

God of grace, we call ourselves disciples of Jesus Christ, yet we confess to creating a Jesus shaped by our own cultural, political, and religious expectations. We want to follow Jesus, but we are a little uncertain, and frankly uncomfortable, with where he may lead us. Open our hearts to where you would have us go, and what you would have us do as disciples. Amen.

2.

REVOLUTIONARY LIFESTYLE

Planning the Session

Session Goals

As a result of conversations and activities connected with this session, group members should begin to:

- explore the question of how challenging the Christian faith is as practiced in their congregation;
- learn about how the church of the first three centuries went from an incendiary illegal movement to an instrument of the state, and the implications for the vibrancy of today's Christian movement;
- express, through the creation of a word cloud, two heresies, and demonstrate an understanding of how these threaten the church today;
- learn about the role of community in establishing and assuring justice;
- encounter more challenging teachings of Jesus;
- explore a deeper commitment to journey with Jesus as disciples.

Biblical Foundation

> *They will rebuild the ancient ruins*
> *and restore the places long devastated;*
> *they will renew the ruined cities*
> *that have been devastated for generations.*
> *(Isaiah 61:4)*

Special Preparation

- Display a simple small cross or picture of a cross. Also continue to provide writing paper and pens for journaling, along with Bibles for those who need them.
- Post the following question on a large sheet of paper or a board: How challenging is the Christianity practiced in our congregation? You will need an additional blank sheet or a board for other activities.
- Provide two large sheets of paper, pencils, and colored markers for the word cloud activity.
- Remember that there are more activities than most groups will have time to complete. As leader, you'll want to go over the session in advance and select or adapt the activities you think will work best for your group in the time allotted.

Getting Started

Opening Activity

As participants arrive, welcome them. Call their attention to the posted question. Invite them to line up along a continuum from "very challenging" on one side of your space to "not challenging at all" on the other side of your space. When everyone has found a place along the continuum line, invite volunteers to explain why they chose to stand where they did. Allow a few minutes for the group to discuss what factors come into play in the life of your congregation to make discipleship more or less challenging. Discuss:

- Is a rigorous, challenging faith appealing to you? Why or why not?

- What does it mean to you to be a disciple of Jesus Christ?

Encourage the group to reflect on the question of how challenging faith is in your congregation as they continue to explore what constitutes a revolutionary lifestyle.

Opening Prayer

O God, we stand in awe of your power and affirm your strength, but we present to the world a domesticated and docile Jesus. We acknowledge that you are in control, but we present to the world a Jesus we can control. We say "Jesus is Lord," but we may act as if "God and country" is our lord. Open our eyes to challenging truths about what it means to follow Jesus. Amen.

Learning Together

Video Study and Discussion

Video Session 2 explores what constitutes a revolutionary lifestyle and how to transform ourselves into radical, risk-taking disciples. Before viewing the segment, invite the group to think about the assertion that Jesus was a rebel and to ponder the question of whether we, too, should be rebels.

After showing the video, discuss the following:

- In response to a question about why men stay away from church, Slaughter suggests it may be due to the benign Jesus the church presents to the world. What do you think of this observation? What other reasons would you give for the absence of men?
- What does Slaughter say is better than the NFL?
- What reason does he give for the fact that the U.S. flag is not displayed at Ginghamsburg Church, and for why he himself does not personally recite the Pledge of Allegiance to the flag?
- What was the potential cost to the believer of the early church for the greeting, "Jesus is Lord"? Why?

Invite the group to read silently Genesis 22:1-19. Ask someone to briefly summarize the story of Abraham and the command to sacrifice Isaac. Discuss:

- In exposing his own children to what he calls the hard places of the world, Slaughter says he came to better understand this story of Abraham and his son Isaac. What do you think he means, and how do you feel about the story and Slaughter's comments?

Suggest that participants make a note in their journals of questions they have after viewing the video. Explain that the group will return to the issues raised in the video and explore them in more depth as they discuss the chapter itself.

Book Study and Discussion

The Taming of the Church

In order to get the context of Acts 17:5-8, a passage discussed in the chapter, invite the group to follow along in their Bibles as a volunteer reads Acts 17:1-8. Then consider the words of the Jews who dragged Paul and Silas before the city officials: "These men . . . have caused trouble all over the world . . ." Ask:

- When did Christians stop causing trouble?

Ask the group to scan the information in the chapter under the heading "The Taming of the Church" and to recall what we learned in the video segment about life for Christians during the first three centuries of the church's history. Invite volunteers to name events that happened prior to A.D. 313 to support their description of life for Christians in that time period. List these events on a large sheet of paper or on a board. Then ask:

- What happened in A.D. 313 that changed life for Christians so drastically?

- In what ways was that event beneficial to the early church? How was it detrimental?

We learn that Constantine in essence made the church an instrument of the state. What he did and what resulted, whether intentional or not, has implications for one of the two heresies the group will now consider.

Explore Two Heresies

Mike Slaughter discusses two heresies that can undermine a wholehearted commitment to Jesus Christ. Form two groups. Assign to one group the heresy of subjugating our allegiance to Christ to any other priority, and assign to the other group the heresy of a privatized faith. Ask each group to read over the information in the chapter about their assigned heresy. They will then create a "word cloud" to explain that heresy.

Each group will post a large sheet of paper and print a phrase describing the heresy in the center of the sheet. Then they will choose words and phrases about the heresy, printing them around the center phrase with colored markers and varying the size, prominence, and frequency of the words to communicate the relative importance of each. The result is a word cloud. After allowing time for groups to work, invite each group to report on the heresy using their word cloud. Discuss:

- How widespread would you say this heresy is today in our culture?
- In what ways does the heresy constitute a threat to a revolutionary lifestyle? If you had to choose one of the two heresies that represents a greater threat, which would it be?

Bible Study and Discussion

Learn about Community

In contrast to the heresy of a privatized religion, we are designed to live and be in community in order to participate in bringing about the new heaven and earth referred to in Revelation 21:1. This is a concept to which the group will return for more in-depth exploration in Session 3. Invite three volunteers to read aloud in turn the following Scriptures: 1 Corinthians 12:12-31; 1 Peter 2:5, 9; and Matthew 5:14-16.

- The term *ekklesia* is often translated as "church," but perhaps a more accurate translation is "the called-out ones." How would you describe your own church community? What is it called to do?
- The Montgomery bus strike was an example of what it means to create a new community of "called-out ones." Do you agree or not? What other examples can you think of?
- What reminder does Slaughter give to his congregants following a baptism, and what does he mean?

Explore More Teachings of Jesus

Practicing a revolutionary lifestyle means fully submitting ourselves to the authority of Jesus' teachings. Ask volunteers to read the following aloud: Matthew 5:31-32; Matthew 7:13-14, 21-23, 24-27, 28-29. Invite them to make observations on these Scriptures and on commentary in the book. Discuss:

- Which of these teachings represent the most challenging words for you personally? Why?
- Slaughter says we are not saved by what we believe but by what we obey. How do you respond?
- What is "Bible idolatry"? What does it mean, and do you believe there is such a thing? What is the difference between the written word and the living Word?

Commit to Lenten Disciplines

- Remind the group of last week's assignment to reread—or read for the first time—one of the Gospels. Recall the two questions they were to consider as they read:

- o How is Jesus presented in this Gospel that is different from your initial impression?
- o As presented in the Gospels, what is Jesus calling you to be and do?
- Ask volunteers who began reading a Gospel to report what they found in their reading and to respond to the first question. As they continue to read that Gospel in the coming week, encourage them to seek further discernment on the second question. Suggest that they record thoughts about this question in their journals.
- We learn that Mike Slaughter has intentionally exposed his children to the world's hard places as a way of passing on the values of the rebel Jesus. Few of us have the connections or the resources to take our children or grandchildren to Dachau or Darfur, but perhaps we can find places in our own communities where the wounds of the world and the need for Christ's healing are evident. Suggest that those in the group with children or grandchildren consider involving them in a church mission project and, further, explaining to them why Jesus calls us to do so.

Wrapping Up

Closing Activity

The Lenten season is a good time to reevaluate our lifestyle and ask ourselves, as a church and as individuals, some challenging questions. Invite the group to consider in silence some of the questions given in the book:

- Where have we accommodated our lives to worldly values instead of Kingdom values, to worldly politics versus a new Kingdom community?
- What are we saying to our children? What are we modeling for our children?
- From what do we need to fast? More importantly, for what do we need to repent?

Invite the group to consider the following questions about your congregation:

- To what values does this church bear witness in its life and practice?
- What does this congregation do to serve as a model for the church's children? How does it do so?
- From what does this congregation need to fast? For what are we in need of repentance?

Encourage the group, after reflecting silently, to note in their journals how they would answer the above questions.

Remind group members to read Chapter 3 before the next session.

Closing Prayer

Slaughter encourages readers to realign their lifestyles with the renegade gospel message. He invites those willing to do so to pray the following prayer, with which we will end the session:

Lord, in the midst of my doubt, skepticism, and uncertainty, I make the commitment today not only to confess you with my lips as Lord Jesus but to go where you are going and do what you are doing. I will leave no route for retreat or escape. I will be called by your name, and I will be numbered among your people. And it is in your name, Jesus, that I pray. Amen.

3.

THE MOST IMPORTANT QUESTION YOU WILL EVER HAVE TO ANSWER

Planning the Session

Session Goals

As a result of conversations and activities connected with this session, group members should begin to:

- examine the historical evidence and statements of skeptics and use the lens of science to explore the identity of Jesus;
- explore Scriptures that reveal the power unleashed in a commitment to community;
- confront and examine their own understanding of who Jesus is;
- further deepen their commitment to journey with Jesus as disciples.

Biblical Foundation

> *Once when Jesus was praying in private and his disciples were with him, he asked them, "Who do the crowds say I am?" They replied, "Some say John the Baptist; others say Elijah; and still others, that one of the prophets of long ago has come back to life." "But what about you?" he asked. "Who do you say I am?" Peter answered, "God's Messiah." (Luke 9:18–20)*

Special Preparation

- Continue to display a simple small cross or picture of a cross, to provide writing paper and pens for journaling, and to bring Bibles for those who need them.
- Get index cards for participants.
- On a large sheet of paper or a board, print a random sampling of responses the video producer received when he asked people the question, "Who is Jesus?" (See the first paragraph of book Chapter 3.)
- Also post the following question: Who is Jesus? And post this response: Peter replied, "You are the eschatological manifestation of the ground of our being, the *kerygma* of which we find the ultimate meaning in our interpersonal relationships." And Jesus said, "What?"
- Locate the hymn "The Summons," found in some denominational hymnals and also online.
- For the closing activity, sketch a vine on a large sheet of paper. Allow enough space for participants to add branches.
- Remember that there are more activities than most groups will have time to complete. As leader, you'll want to go over the session in advance and select or adapt the activities you think will work best for your group in the time allotted.

Getting Started

Opening Activity

As participants arrive, welcome them. Call their attention to the posted list of responses to the question, "Who is Jesus?"

Distribute index cards and pens and invite group members to reflect on the question, then to print their own response on the card. Encourage them not simply to jot down an answer one expects from churchgoers, but to give it serious thought and then to express what they honestly believe, even if their response is, "I'm not sure."

When everyone has had a chance to respond, ask participants to set aside their cards and let the group know you will suggest a way to use them later in the session. Tell the group that in this session they will grapple with how people and groups across the centuries have attempted to define Jesus, as well as how they themselves articulate who he is, and what difference it makes in their lives and in how they live as disciples.

Opening Prayer

Eternal God, we affirm with words the gift of your Son, Jesus. We acknowledge that in him you came among us in human form. Yet our lives do not always reflect where our true allegiance lies. And if we are honest, we confess we sometimes have doubts about just who this Jesus is. By your spirit, help us to confront our indecision. Sharpen our commitment, we pray. In the name of the rebel Jesus. Amen.

Learning Together

Video Study and Discussion

Video Session 3 addresses what has been called the most important question you will ever have to answer: Who is Jesus? Before viewing the video, invite participants to reflect on how they themselves responded to the question in the opening activity.

After showing the video, discuss the following:

- C. S. Lewis observed that we must decide if Jesus is a liar, a lunatic, or Lord. What reasons did Lewis give for asserting that Jesus must be identified in one and only one of those three ways? How do you respond to his assertion?

- For you, what is the most compelling argument as to why God had to come in human form? What, if anything, does suffering have to do with it?
- Why does Slaughter say that Christianity is the one religion you can't do alone? What do you think he means in saying that shared brokenness becomes a strength?
- In the video, a recovered crack addict named Lori tells her story. What can we learn from Lori's experience of recovery, even including her relapse?

Invite anyone willing to do so to tell about how he or she gained strength through experiencing community. Was there a person or persons whose shared experience helped them to say, "If that person can make it, then I can too"? Encourage participants to note the questions they thought of while watching the video and to jot these down in their journals.

Book Study and Discussion

The Case for the Lordship of Jesus

Ask a volunteer to read aloud today's biblical foundation, Luke 9:18-20. Call the group's attention to the response you posted before class and read it aloud. Say that this joke has made the rounds in various forms. It points up how people of many perspectives, even theologians, struggle with how to identify Jesus.

Form two groups. Invite one group to create a list of statements they have heard people make, or arguments they have heard people use, in denying that Jesus was who he claimed to be. For example, people sometimes say that Jesus was just a good moral teacher. Ask the other group to draw up a list of arguments that could be used in asserting Jesus was who he claimed to be.

When the groups have finished their work, have each group report to the large group. Discuss:

- In your opinion, does the evidence make a compelling argument for who Jesus is—or is not?

- Slaughter observes that he has often been criticized for not issuing more altar calls. What is his explanation?
- In both the video and the text, we learn what a rabbi was in biblical times and how a rabbi's disciples were expected to follow the day-to-day routines of his life, not just during formal times of teaching. We read that the disciples were urged to be "covered in the dust of your Rabbi." How do you think this information affects or could affect our acceptance of an institutionalized, Sunday school Jesus?

Bible Study and Discussion

The Importance of Community

Christianity is a faith that you can't do alone; it grows most vibrantly in the context of community. Invite the group to turn to Luke 9:10-17, the story of the feeding of the five thousand. Note that this account comes just before the passage in which Jesus asks who the disciples say that he is. Then ask the group to follow along as a volunteer reads the story aloud. Afterward, ask the group to scan the paragraphs in Chapter 3 that deal with the passage. Discuss:

- What do we learn in these passages about the power of multiplication?
- What examples can you cite from your own experiences in community? Why is *only* a limiting word?

Exploring God's Heart Revealed in Jesus

Jesus gives flesh and reality to a God who cares, loves us deeply, and is willing to die to save us. With your group, continue to explore the heart of God by discussing some sayings and parables of Jesus. Form three small groups to consider the three parables found in Luke 15: the lost sheep, the lost coin, and the lost son (often called the prodigal son or wayward son). Ask each group to read their assigned parable; then ask each group to respond to the following:

- In this parable, Jesus describes God as . . .
- What does this parable tell you about Jesus? If Jesus is "God with skin on," what does the parable tell us about Jesus?

Continue Lenten Disciplines

- Remind the group of their continuing assignment to reread—or read for the first time—one of the Gospels. In what ways is this reading helping them answer this most important question: Who is Jesus? As group members continue to read the Gospels, encourage them to deepen their understanding of what it means that Jesus is Lord and what it means to follow him. Suggest that they record thoughts about this question in their journals.
- Ask someone to read aloud Luke 14:16-24. Note that the three excuses the servants made are the same ones we often use when we avoid following Jesus: allegiance to our material property, our work, and our relationships. Encourage participants to pray in the coming week for discernment about how their actions and commitments might be realigned so they can be more faithful disciples.
- Encourage participants to take home the index cards on which they responded to the question, "Who is Jesus?" Suggest that they use the cards as prayer prompts, inviting God's Spirit to guide them into a deeper understanding of Jesus' identity and significance. Ask them also to pray for discernment about how they might commit more fully to real discipleship.

Wrapping Up

Closing Activities

The Metaphor of the Vine

Call attention to the sheet with the vine that you prepared before class. Ask someone to read aloud John 15:1-6. Invite the group to think about this metaphor for community. Ask the following, encouraging brief responses and suggesting that group members continue to reflect about them on their own:

- Jesus says those who abide in him will bear fruit. What does it mean to abide in him? How can you be a fruitful disciple?
- Jesus says that the Father prunes the branches to make them bear more fruit. What do you think he means by pruning? What are the implications for discipleship?
- What happens to branches that do not bear fruit? What happens to a branch that is not a part of the vine? What does this mean for us?

Invite participants to add a branch to the vine and label it with their name, as a reminder to follow Jesus and to abide with him in community.

Remind group members to read Chapter 3 before the next session, and to continue reading at least one Gospel account in its entirety.

Sing Together

Sing or recite the hymn "The Summons" or show an online video of a performance. Alternatively, invite the group to recite the Apostles' Creed, found at the end of the chapter.

Closing Prayer

Gracious God, you know our innermost thoughts. Though we may be able to hide them from others, you know the doubts and uncertainties that plague our faith journeys. Lead us, with Peter, to proclaim that Jesus is the Christ sent from God. By your spirit, lead us to respond more faithfully to the call of discipleship. Make us witnesses to the miracle of multiplication as we combine with others to place our gifts, resources, and lives in your hands. Amen.

4.

SEEING JESUS TODAY

Planning the Session

Session Goals

As a result of conversations and activities connected with this session, group members should begin to:

- encounter the power of expectancy and examine the role of persistence in actively seeking Christ's presence and listening for Christ's voice;
- explore teachings of Jesus that help answer the questions: What do we need to do to see and experience Jesus today? When do we see Jesus? Where do we find Jesus today?
- learn more about the role of the community and the presence of the Holy Spirit in bringing more clarity about God's will for our lives;
- discover reasons we fail to see Jesus today;
- be introduced to how one's life mission leads to meeting, experiencing, and following Jesus;
- further deepen their commitment to journey with Jesus as disciples.

Biblical Foundation

> *"Ask and it will be given to you; seek and you will find; knock and the door will be opened to you. For everyone who asks receives; the one who seeks finds; and to the one who knocks, the door will be opened."*
>
> *(Matthew 7:7-8)*

> *"Sir," they said, "we would like to see Jesus."*
> *(John 12:21)*

Special Preparation

- Continue to display a simple small cross or picture of a cross, and to provide writing paper and pens for journaling and Bibles for those who need them.
- Download from the Internet some pictures with optical illusions showing images hidden within images (such as the classic face and vase), and either project these images or print them off. If possible, find some images that include Jesus.
- Get hymnals with the hymn "Open My Eyes, That I May See" or download the lyrics from an Internet site.
- On individual index cards or slips of paper, make several copies of the following terms: *car games, CD, glasses, hardness of heart, spiritual drowsiness.* Create enough cards that each participant can have one.
- Get copies of current newspapers, or download news stories from Internet news sites. Provide colored paper and markers.
- This session uses the metaphors of vision and hearing to explore how we encounter Jesus in unexpected places if we seek him. If you have a participant with limited vision, you may want to use an alternative to the opening activity, one that focuses on how our expectations can limit how we understand an issue.
- Remember that there are more activities than most groups will have time to complete. As leader, you'll want to go over

the session in advance and select—or adapt—the activities you think will work best for your group in the time allotted.

Getting Started

Opening Activity

As participants arrive, welcome them. Tell the group that you are going to show them some pictures and ask them to look for images contained in the pictures. Quickly project one or more optical illusions (or show the printed image) and invite the group to tell what they see. For the face and vase illusion, many may report seeing the face, but some may see other images in the illusion. After discussing the images, project or show them again and invite the group to look for the image they did not initially see. Discuss:

- What do you think influenced the image you saw first? What did you expect to see?
- Why do you think you initially did not see the other image?

Tell the group that in this session, we will explore the power of expectancy and how it affects where we encounter and experience Jesus.

Sing or recite together the hymn "Open My Eyes, That I May See."

Opening Prayer

Open our eyes, O God. In the words of the hymn, open them to glimpses of truth. Open our ears, O God, for voices of truth. Silently now we wait for thee—ready, O God, thy will to see. Open our eyes, open our ears—illumine us, Spirit divine. Amen.

Learning Together

Video Study and Discussion

The Session 4 video asks the question "Are you looking for Jesus?" and examines the power of expectancy. We discuss looking for Jesus in the most unlikely places and, as a result, finding purpose.

Before viewing the video, invite participants to think of a time when they were looking for a lost item, only to later find it in plain view. Ask:

- Why was the item so hard to find when it was clearly visible? In what way do you think your expectation about where it was played a part in overlooking it?

After showing the video, discuss the following:

- Slaughter suggests that in John 14:14, the phrase "in my name" is key. What does he mean?
- Slaughter asks, "How could I see the sedan and not the Sudan?" To what is he referring? What does it have to do with expectancy?
- What is the role of persistence in addressing so-called compassion fatigue?

Slaughter asserts that it is God's will that children should not live in poverty. He notes that 33 percent of his community's children live below the poverty line. Challenge the group to find out what that percentage is in your community. Ask them to pray about and reflect on what God's will for those children is, and what God might be calling group members to do about it. Invite them to continue thinking about what questions were raised for them during the video and to jot these down in their journals.

Bible Study and Discussion

Seek and You Shall Find

Invite someone to read aloud one of the biblical foundation Scriptures, Matthew 7:7-8. In the video, a woman remarks that what the Scripture affirms—that we will receive what we ask for and find what we seek—never seems to work that way for her. "What am I missing?" she asks. Ask the group to discuss the woman's question.

Note that the Greek verbs in the Matthew passage are in the present continuous tense. Have someone reread the passage to reflect that. ("Ask and keep on asking . . .") Then ask:

- How do you think Christians can sustain that kind of persistence? What spiritual practices do you think might undergird an attitude of actively seeking Christ's presence and listening for Christ's voice?

Community and the Holy Spirit

Ask a volunteer to read aloud John 14:15-19. Then ask the group to scan the information about the passage in book Chapter 4 (beginning with "In John 14:15-17, Jesus made a promise ..."). Remind the group that in Session 3 they were introduced to a heresy, that of privatized religion, and explored the importance of community in the Christian life.

Ask someone to read Matthew 18:19-20. On a board, print the phrases "Where two or three gather" and "in my name." Discuss:

- What is the connection between community and the presence of the Holy Spirit?
- If the phrase "in my name" indicates that something is aligned with God's will, in what ways might being in community open us to more clarity about God's will for our lives?

Explore Parables

Form small groups of three people each to explore the parables and teachings in Matthew 25. In each group, assign to one person the parable of the bridesmaids (verses 1-13), another the parable of the talents (verses 14-30), and the third the passage about the judgment of the nations (verses 31-46). Ask group members to read their passage and scan the relevant information in the book chapter. Then ask them to summarize their passage and explain for the other two in their group the relevance of the passage to seeing and experiencing Jesus. Allow time for small-group discussion, then ask the large group to respond to the following:

- What do we need to do to see and experience Jesus today?
- When do we see Jesus?
- Where do we find Jesus today?

Book Study and Discussion

Reasons We Fail to See Jesus

Point out that in book Chapter 3, the group explored the question, "Who do you say that I am?" In Chapter 4, the group will examine the questions of when we see Jesus and why we sometimes fail to do so.

Invite the group to join in a scavenger hunt in the book chapter. Distribute the index cards you prepared before the session. Ask the group to scan the text and find the item or phrase referenced on their card and be prepared to explain its significance in explaining why we sometimes fail to see Jesus. They can then tell the anecdote Slaughter recounted related to that item and, if possible, give an example from their own experience.

As participants name the reasons revealed by the various examples, list the reasons on a board or a large piece of paper.

Reasons might include:

- faulty expectations;
- our own lack of faith or faith restrictions;
- our hardness of heart;
- trying to find Jesus in the extraordinary rather than the ordinary;
- spiritual drowsiness.

Invite a volunteer or two to comment on a time when one of these reasons prevented them from seeing Jesus. Also ask the group to consider if there are other reasons they can think of that may have limited their ability to see Jesus and experience his power.

Finding Our BHAG

Mike Slaughter refers in the chapter to his BHAG—big hairy audacious goal (or God-purpose), a term used by Jim Collins and Jerry Porras in their book *Built to Last: Successful Habits of Visionary Companies* and adapted by Slaughter in his book *Dare to Dream: Creating a God-Sized Mission Statement for Your Life*. Discuss:

- Slaughter contends that when we get serious about Jesus Christ and our BHAG, Jesus will completely mess up our lives and our preconceived notions about what life is supposed to be. Looking back on your faith journey, where can you see evidence of God's voice, however indistinct? How did you respond? If you have not had that experience, what are some ways you might be more aware of your God-purpose?
- Will Willimon and Stanley Hauerwas contend in their book *Resident Aliens* that we cannot know Jesus without following Jesus—that, in a sense, we follow Jesus before we know him. Would you agree or disagree that following comes

first? Could following and knowing be in the present continuous tense, like Jesus' words in Matthew?

Continue Lenten Disciplines

- Ask group members to report on where they are in their continuing assignment to read a Gospel account. Some members of the group may have completed reading one Gospel. If so, encourage them to begin reading another account. Point out that each Gospel writer was addressing his account to a particular community of Christians. If participants have completed Mark's Gospel—the earliest Gospel in the New Testament—they may find it interesting to read the Gospel of John, the latest of the four Gospels, addressed to a community of Christians experiencing persecution for their faith.
- Although viewing a film may seem like an unusual Lenten discipline, invite participants to consider renting a copy of the film *Bruce Almighty* and looking for how their understanding of who God is might be expanded.

Wrapping Up

Closing Activity

In the video and in the chapter, Slaughter describes how an encounter with the newspaper opened his eyes to the needs in Darfur. Distribute copies of a recent newspaper or stories from Internet news sites to participants. Invite them to find headlines of stories that speak to the wounds of the world in your own community and in the nation. Ask them to mark and mount these stories on sheets of colored paper. Invite each participant to read aloud the headline he or she found. Post the sheets of paper on a board and invite the group to consider them in silence. Encourage the group to think about where they might see Jesus in each story.

Remind participants to read Chapter 5 before the next session.

Closing Prayer

Tell participants that Chapter 4 closes with the prayer the Apostle Paul offered for believers in Ephesus, with which you will also close this session.

I pray that the God of our Lord Jesus Christ, the Father of glory, will give you a spirit of wisdom and revelation that makes God known to you. I pray that the eyes of your heart will have enough light to see what is the hope of God's call, what is the richness of God's glorious inheritance among believers, and what is the overwhelming greatness of God's power that is working among us believers. (Ephesians 1:17-19 CEB)

5.

THE WAY
OF THE CROSS

Planning the Session

Session Goals

As a result of conversations and activities connected with this session, group members should begin to:

- explore the contrast between *chronos* and *kairos* time and discover how Jesus, understanding the limits of his chronos time, resolutely set about to accomplish his kairos mission.
- experience a reminder of the limitations of our own chronos time;
- explore the shape and demands of obedient discipleship through an interactive journey alongside Jesus as he encountered people on the way to Jerusalem;
- expand their understanding of what it means to take up your cross and follow Jesus;
- further deepen their commitment to journey with Jesus as disciples.

Biblical Foundation

> *"Whoever wants to be my disciple must deny them-*
> *selves and take up their cross daily and follow me."*
>> *(Luke 9:23)*

> *In your relationships with one another, have the same*
> *mindset as Christ Jesus:*
>> *Who, being in very nature God,*
>>> *did not consider equality with God something*
>>> *to be used to his own advantage;*
>> *rather, he made himself nothing*
>>> *by taking the very nature of a servant,*
>>> *being made in human likeness.*
>> *And being found in appearance as a man,*
>>> *he humbled himself*
>>> *by becoming obedient to death—*
>>>> *even death on a cross!*
>>> *(Philippians 2:5-8)*

Special Preparation

- Continue to display a small simple cross or picture of a cross and to provide materials for journaling and Bibles for those who did not bring one.
- On a large sheet of paper, make a chart listing the following: oxygen (65%), carbon (18.5%), hydrogen (9.5%), nitrogen (3%), calcium, phosphorus, potassium, sulfur, sodium, chlorine, magnesium.
- Post the following open-ended prompt: "At this time of the year ten years ago, I was …"
- Get a small bowl of ashes.
- For this session, Bible and book study are combined in an interactive "Journey with Jesus" to explore the shape and demands of obedient discipleship. In addition to the directions in the session, you will need the following: for

all three stations, large sheet of paper on which you will print the directions (see below). For Station 1: a variety of art materials to construct "idols"; Station 2: large sheets of paper and markers. Set up the stations at intervals around the room. If you like, also place a battery-operated candle at each station.

- If you choose not to create the Journey with Jesus, simply use the questions at the end of the activity to stimulate discussion. If time allows, have participants also read and discuss the additional Scriptures under each heading.
- You will need three large sheets of paper and markers for the closing activity. Label each of the sheets with one of three kingdoms mentioned in the chapter: Kingdom of Pilate, Kingdom of Jesus, and Kingdom of the Religious Elite.
- Get the hymn "I Have Decided to Follow Jesus" from a hymnal or Internet site.
- Remember that there are more activities than most groups will have time to complete. As leader, you'll want to go over the session in advance and select or adapt the activities you think will work best for your group in the time allotted.

Getting Started

Opening Activity

As participants arrive, welcome them. Call their attention to the list of elements you have posted, and ask if anyone can identify what these elements in these percentages comprise. Someone will likely identify it as the chemical composition of the human body. (There are trace amounts of other elements as well.) Tell the group that, on average, eight chemical elements comprise the majority of the mineral matter in soils: oxygen, silicon, aluminum, iron, magnesium, calcium, sodium, and potassium, with trace amounts of more than eighty other elements. Ask:

- What do you notice about the elements in dirt compared with the elements that comprise the human body?

Form pairs and invite participants to respond to the open-ended prompt you posted. ("At this time of the year ten years ago, I was …") After allowing a few minutes for pairs to discuss, ask volunteers to tell where they were and what they were doing. Remind the group that there are two kinds of time. *Chronos*, from which the word *chronological* comes, is quantitative time—the time participants were just discussing. Ask:

- What is *kairos* time? What do you think a kairos mission might be? What do you believe your kairos mission is?

Ask someone to tell what Ash Wednesday is. Remind the group that in many Christian churches across the span of denominations, Christians are marked on the forehead with the sign of the cross using ashes from the previous Palm Sunday's palms. This is a reminder that earth is not our permanent residence; we are here on temporary assignment. In this session, participants will explore how Jesus, knowing how limited his chronos time was, resolutely set about to accomplish his kairos mission.

Pass around the bowl of ashes you brought, inviting participants to reflect on the Scripture sometimes used on Ash Wednesday: ". . . for dust you are and to dust you will return" (Genesis 3:19).

Opening Prayer

Gracious God, we acknowledge that few of us can know how we will end or how many days of chronos time we have left. In your time, we know that a human life is nothing but a puff of air. Yet we can affirm that we know from whom we came and to whom we will return. Strengthen our resolute commitment to the journey, that we may live into our own role in fulfilling God's kairos mission, take up our cross, and follow Jesus Christ. Amen.

Learning Together

Video Study and Discussion

The Session 5 video explores the cross and what it means to be a living sacrifice. Before viewing the video, invite the group to reflect on these words from book Chapter 5:

> *To make the declaration "Jesus is Lord" means an all-in, whole life commitment to follow Jesus in an alternative, sacrificial way of life, fully pledging one's allegiance to the rebel Jesus in faithfully serving the renegade gospel.*

After viewing the video, discuss the following:

- In response to a question about what it means to pick up your cross daily and follow Jesus, Slaughter responds that the cross is not a burden; the cross means death. What does he mean? What is the connection between baptism and death? To what do we need to die?
- In referring to the hard personal work that must be done to be a radical follower of Jesus Christ, Slaughter observes that there is no way to be transformed without doing the "God painful stuff." What do you think he means? What spiritual practices might help you as you move through Lent, a time of denial and introspection?

Continue to encourage participants to think about the questions raised in their own minds as they watch the video. Encourage them to jot these down in their journals.

Bible and Book Study and Discussion

Journey with Jesus

Invite a volunteer to read aloud one of this session's biblical foundation passages, Philippians 2:5-8. Jesus' encounters with people in his final weeks illuminate the meaning of the cross and what it means to follow him in obedient discipleship.

Tell the group that for some Christians, walking the stations of the cross is a tradition during Holy Week. While the group will not be replicating that practice, in this session they will walk alongside Jesus for a portion of his journey with the cross and in so doing explore the shape and demands of obedient discipleship. Depending on the size of your group, either form three smaller groups and have each group begin with a different station, or travel with Jesus as one large group. Tell participants that they will need the study book, their journals, and their Bibles. Ask them to move to their assigned station, read the sign, and do the activities:

Station 1

- Have someone read aloud Luke 9:57-62.
- Silently scan the information in book Chapter 5 under the heading "Do You Understand What You Are Signing Up For?"
- Note the following in your journal for later reflection: Write down your consumer debt. How does it compare with what you give to the church?
- Use the art materials to make an image of something that threatens to become your materialistic idol.

Station 2

- Have someone read aloud Luke 9:59-60.
- Silently scan the information in book Chapter 5 under the heading "The Cross Challenges the Priority of Our Relationships."
- On a large sheet of paper, draw three concentric circles. Inside the first circle, print the names of family members who are your closest relationships. Inside the next circle out, print the names of close friends. In the outside circle, print the names of work colleagues, acquaintances, and those with whom you relate on committees, in recreational

activities, and the like. Consider how prioritizing Jesus first can make for greater health in all your relationships. Make a note in your journal.

Station 3
- Have someone read aloud Luke 9:61.
- Silently scan the information in book Chapter 5 under the heading "The Cross Challenges Our Indecisiveness."
- Reflect on how you might answer the call to discipleship: "To act justly and to love mercy and to walk humbly with your God" (Micah 6:8). Record those thoughts in your journal.

When participants have completed the journey with Jesus, debrief the experience. Invite them to make any general comments or raise any questions that emerged on the journey. Discuss some of the following:

- What reasons does Slaughter give for intentionally choosing not to use the term *volunteer*? What is your response to his assertion that we sometimes present ourselves in the church as volunteers rather than as servants? Does this term change your perception of how you might offer your gifts of time and talents in the faith community? If so, in what way?
- In what specific ways might you use your affluence for the purpose of influence, as an aid to those who have neither?
- Sometimes we allow relationships to become an excuse for not acting on God's will. Can you name an example of how this might happen in your own life?
- Jesus made it painfully clear that we cannot follow the living God in the way of the cross and serve the expectations of a spiritually dead person at the same time. How do you respond?
- When Dr. Martin Luther King, Jr., began the Birmingham Campaign in 1963, he met resistance from clergy who contended the fight against segregation should be waged in

the courts, not on the streets. King's response was chillingly prophetic for the church today. Would you agree? Why or why not?

- Name some areas where you believe the church today, or you yourself, struggle with personal prejudices and self-serving agendas.

Continue Lenten Disciplines

- Ask group members to report on where they are in their continuing assignment to read a Gospel account.
- Lent is a focused period of personal reflection and repentance through prayer, Scripture reading, and fasting during which we lay aside things we ordinarily enjoy (such as sugar, alcohol, television, or social media) and reevaluate our faith journey by asking some hard questions. In the coming week, invite the group to reflect in their journals on the following questions:
  o Does my faith talk match my faith walk?
  o Am I trying to live with a foot in two contradictory worlds?
  o Am I putting off until tomorrow what God is calling me to do today?
  o Am I offering myself to Jesus as a volunteer who serves when convenient or a servant who acts sacrificially?

Wrapping Up

Closing Activity

Call attention to the sheets of paper you prepared that are headed with the three kingdoms referred to in the book: Kingdom of Pilate, Kingdom of Jesus, and Kingdom of the Religious Elite. Form three smaller groups, assigning one kingdom to each, and ask each group to scan silently the material in book Chapter 5 under the heading "Kingdoms on a Collision

Course" that is related to their kingdom. Ask each group to jot down on their sheet some information describing their kingdom. In the large group, ask each smaller group to report briefly. Discuss:

- Why does Slaughter say these kingdoms were on collision course?
- What factors led to Jesus' arrest and death?
- If the church truly embraced what it means to say "Jesus is Lord," with what present-day "kingdoms" might disciples of Christ be in danger of colliding? What might be the risks entailed in this kind of discipleship?
- After studying this chapter, what would you say it means to take up your cross and follow Jesus?

Sing or recite together the hymn "I Have Decided to Follow Jesus." If you use an Internet video, invite participants to reflect on the images used in the video and consider what images they might have chosen to communicate what it means to be a radical follower of Jesus.

Remind group members to read Chapter 6 before the next session.

Closing Prayer

Gracious God, we know that we cannot experience resurrection to the miracle of abundant life here and life everlasting until we put to death our self-determination. Guide us, we pray, as we seek to give ourselves ever more fully and sacrificially to the concerns of your heart. In the name of Jesus Christ we pray. Amen.

6.

RESURRECTION

Planning the Session

Session Goals

As a result of conversations and activities connected with this session, group members should begin to:

- discover the significance of the Resurrection accounts in the four Gospels;
- explore the claims for Jesus' resurrection;
- examine the faith/doubt struggle;
- explore the importance of committing one's faith, however small, to action;
- examine three action verbs in Jesus' directive to his disciples—*look, touch,* and *see*—and learn how these relate to dealing with doubts;
- extend faith practices beyond the season of Lent to continue the journey with Jesus as disciples;
- evaluate how their image of Jesus has evolved through the study and celebrate its transformative power.

Biblical Foundation

> *But if it is preached that Christ has been raised from the dead, how can some of you say that there is no resurrection of the dead? If there is no resurrection of the dead, then not even Christ has been raised. And if Christ has not been raised, our preaching is useless and so is your faith. (1 Corinthians 15:12-14)*

Special Preparation

- Continue to display a small simple cross or picture of a cross and to provide materials for journaling and Bibles for those who did not bring one.
- On a large sheet of paper or a board, print the following excerpt from the Apostles' Creed (Traditional Version):

> *[I believe] in Jesus Christ his only Son our Lord: who was conceived by the Holy Spirit, born of the Virgin Mary, suffered under Pontius Pilate, was crucified, dead, and buried; the third day he rose from the dead; he ascended into heaven...* [1]

- Head each of three large sheets of paper with one of the following: Look—at the Credible Evidence; Touch—Invitation to Involvement; and See—Through the Eyes of the Risen Christ. Provide markers for each sheet.
- Gather the materials for participants to make a simple cross of their own, such as large nails and wire.
- Have available again the images of Jesus from Session 1, either digitally to project or printed in hard copy.
- Again get hymnals with the hymn "Open My Eyes, That I May See," or download the lyrics from an Internet site.
- Remember that there are more activities than most groups will have time to complete. As leader, you'll want to go over the session in advance and select or adapt the activities you think will work best for your group in the time allotted.

Getting Started

Opening Activity

As participants arrive, welcome them and randomly assign to each person one of the four Gospels. Ask them to page through and estimate approximately how much of their Gospel is devoted to the account of Jesus' arrest, trial, crucifixion, and resurrection. After allowing some time for participants to examine their Gospel accounts, invite volunteers to tell what they found.

In the study book, point out the quotation from British theologian N. T. Wright, and have someone read it aloud. Then ask the question below. Here is the quotation:

> *Take away the stories of Jesus's birth, and you lose only two chapters of Matthew and two of Luke. Take away the resurrection, and you lose the entire New Testament and most of the second-century fathers as well.*[2]

- What conclusions can we draw when we compare the amount of the four Gospels devoted to Jesus' birth with the amount devoted to the account of the events leading up to his crucifixion and resurrection?

Note that First Corinthians was written no more than thirty years after Jesus' resurrection. Have someone read aloud 1 Corinthians 15:3-6. Ask:

- Do you find this early testimony about Jesus' resurrection compelling? Why or why not?
- What else can you cite about the early years of the Christian movement that seem to you to be important clues about whether the Resurrection is real?

Ask the group to reflect silently on how they themselves would answer the question of whether they believe in the physical resurrection of Jesus Christ. Would they answer no, yes, or sometimes? In this session, they will explore the claims for Jesus' resurrection, as well as the doubts that plague most of us at least part of the time.

Opening Prayer

Eternal God, we want to believe, and yet for some of us, doubts can creep in. In a rational culture in which scientific truth governs our day-to-day life, the reality of resurrection can seem astonishing. It is sometimes hard to embrace a truth that cannot be fully explained! Open our hearts to the movement of your Spirit this day. In the name of the resurrected Christ. Amen.

Learning Together

Video Study and Discussion

The Session 6 video addresses the radical implications of the Resurrection and how to deal with the doubts that hold us back from our God-created purpose.

Before viewing the video, invite the group to read aloud the excerpt from the Apostles' Creed from the posted sheet that you prepared before class. Ask that they pause briefly at the spaces (ellipses or dots) to reflect on what they themselves believe about Jesus and his resurrection.

After viewing the video, discuss the following questions about Jesus' resurrection:

- How does Mike Slaughter differentiate between historical and scientific evidence?
- What is the significance of eyewitnesses to the Resurrection?

Slaughter discusses how to deal with doubt. Ask:

- In speaking of his own doubts, what does Slaughter say is his prayer?

- Why does Slaughter say Jesus made Peter a leader of the young church?
- Why is the mustard seed such a good metaphor for faith?
- Where does Slaughter say God does God's best work? Where do you say?

Invite the group to continue reflecting on the extent to which they are willing to act, even in the midst of doubts. Tell them that the conversation in the video about the three verbs in the risen Christ's directive to his disciples will be explored in more depth later in the session.

Book and Bible Study and Discussion

Exploring the Quality of Faith

Invite the group to turn to Mark 9:14-29, and ask a volunteer to read the passage aloud. As the group heard in the video, the prayer of the father has become Mike Slaughter's daily prayer mantra because it expresses the tension between faith and doubt in his own faith journey. Discuss:

- Faith and doubt seem to go together. In your own experience, is this true? Can you describe a time in your life when you experienced a dark night of the soul?

Jesus' words about mustard seed faith remind us that it's not about how much faith you have, but how much you commit to action. Discuss:

- What does Slaughter mean when he says the Resurrection defines the new possible? What does it mean that the impossible is the new possible?
- Consider examples of some people who defied conventional wisdom to make accomplishments that have contributed

to human advancement. Some might call this thinking out of the box. What does it mean for Christians to think "out of the grave"?

- What practices would you say are essential for nurturing the mustard seed of your faith?
- The Introduction to the study book quotes from *Resident Aliens*, a book by Will Willimon and Stanley Hauerwas, who say we cannot know Jesus without following Jesus. How does this relate to acting on the level of faith we have?

Call the group's attention to the description in Chapter 6 (under the heading "Dealing with Doubt") of findings by the Pew Forum on Religion and Public Life about the rapid spread of Christianity in the developing world. Pose this question:

- Christian faith seems to flourish in times and places where people face persecution and doubt? Why do you think this is?

While Christians do not face persecution in the U.S., we do face a more subtle and perhaps more insidious threat to our faith—our highly secularized, consumer oriented, materialistic culture. Note that in decades past, most people with whom Christians might interact were Christians themselves, and churchgoing was considered a key activity for most.

Ask participants to consider the context of their lives—the workplace, schools, recreational activities in which they regularly engage. Discuss:

- In your own day-to-day life, are most people with whom you interact Christians, of some other faith, or nonreligious?
- What is, or might be, the response of people if you act out of a radical commitment to Jesus Christ?

Dealing with Doubt

Recall the three action verbs in Jesus' directive to his disciples: look, touch, and see. Then invite participants to read silently the Resurrection account in Luke 24:1-12 and the walk to Emmaus account in verses 13-35. Then ask someone to read aloud verses 36-43.

Ask participants to read silently the information in the study book under the headings "Look—at the Credible Evidence"; "Touch—Invitation to Involvement"; and "See—Through the Eyes of the Resurrected Christ." Call attention to the three sheets of paper you prepared before class with these three headings, and ask group members to select one of the three topics to discuss with others in the group and to form three groups for that purpose. Suggest that conversation in the three groups be broadened to include information from the video segments and from other parts of Chapter 6. Ask each group to formulate three or more questions to pose to the large group and to write the questions on the sheets.

Allow several minutes for each group to work; then gather again as a large group. Ask each small group in turn to pose its questions, and discuss together. Then ask:

- Which of Jesus' directives to his disciples is the most helpful to you in dealing with your doubts?

Extending Lenten Disciplines

Invite group members to respond to the following:

- In attempting to read an entire Gospel from beginning to end, I was most surprised by ...
- I was most troubled by ...
- My view of Jesus was transformed in this way ...

- Remind the group that, although the season of Lent is coming to its conclusion, some of the practices in which they engaged can be extended, such as reading an additional Gospel account.

Encourage group members to engage in regular Bible study if they have not already been doing so. Also suggest that they continue journaling as a way to reflect on their faith.

Invite the group to refer back to the questions they have listed while viewing the videos. Many of these questions could be grist for further group discussion or might be addressed to the pastor.

Wrapping Up

Closing Activities

Celebrate the Rebel Jesus

Once again project images of Jesus, or pass around printed images of Jesus, that were used in the first session. Ask group members to reflect on how their understanding of the rebel Jesus and his revolutionary message has changed in the course of the study. Then ask them to describe how the encounter with this Jesus has given them new eyes and a new Resurrection worldview, one that may change how they view themselves and others.

Create a Cross

Call the group's attention to the cross you have been displaying for the duration of the study. While many churches have crosses on prominent display, oftentimes these crosses are elaborate and expensive. Distribute the materials you have gathered for making small crosses (such as large nails and lengths of wire) and invite participants to create a simple cross. Encourage participants to use this cross as a reminder of what it means to take up one's cross and, with a radical faith, follow the rebel Jesus.

Sing or recite together the hymn "Open My Eyes, That I May See"

Closing Prayer

Read this prayer, with which Mike Slaughter closes the study and that he invites us to pray with him.

Lord, by no means do I fully comprehend who you are. But I commit today to give my life to you . . . not just in words, but in action. With all my imperfections, I accept your love and forgiveness, and I extend it to others. I pledge my allegiance to the rebel Jesus and commit myself to the renegade gospel. Not my will but your will be done. In Jesus' name. Amen.

NOTES

1. "The Apostles' Creed, Traditional Version," *The United Methodist Hymnal* (Nashville: The United Methodist Publishing House, 1989), 881.

2. Wright, N. T., *Surprised by Hope: Rethinking Heaven, the Resurrection, and the Mission of the Church* (New York: HarperOne, 2008), 43.